RICK AND BUBBA'S
BIG HONKIN'
BOOK OF
HUNTIN'

OTHER RICK AND BUBBA BOOKS

Rick and Bubba's Expert Guide to God, Country,
Family, and Anything Else We Can Think Of

The Rick and Bubba Code

Rick and Bubba for President

RICK AND BUBBA'S
BIG HONKIN'
BOOK OF
HUNTIN'

with Martha Bolton

THOMAS NELSON
Since 1798

NASHVILLE   DALLAS   MEXICO CITY   RIO DE JANEIRO   BEIJING

We would like to dedicate this book to game wardens everywhere. Thank you for your hard work to ensure that we can enjoy hunting and fishing for generations to come.

Published in Nashville, Tennessee, by Thomas Nelson. Thomas Nelson is a registered trademark of Thomas Nelson, Inc.

Punblished in association with the literary agency of Sanford Communications, Inc., Portland, Oregon.

Illustrations by Trevor Stone Irvin of Irvin Productions: www.irvinproductions.net

Thomas Nelson, Inc., titles may be purchased in bulk for educational, business, fund-raising, or sales promotional use. For information, please e-mail SpecialMarkets@ThomasNelson.com.

Library of Congress Cataloging-in-Publication Data

ISBN 978-1-4016-0401-1

Printed in the United States of America

08 09 10 11 12 WOR 5 4 3 2 1

TABLE OF CONTENTS

RICK · BUBBA ·

INTRODUCTION

You are holding it in your hands—the last word on hunting. Yes, *Rick and Bubba's Big Honkin' Book of Huntin'* supersedes all others that have gone before it. Between these covers you will find everything you have ever wanted to know about the sport of hunting . . . and maybe a few things you didn't.

If renowned hunting book author Jeff Foxworthy—or anyone else for that matter—wants to challenge us on our "last word on hunting" claim, we'll gladly take them on. All they have to do is look at our publishing date (which is later than theirs) and we can prove that because our book came last, it is the last word on the subject. Of course, if someone else comes along and writes a hunting book after ours, then he or she will have the last word on hunting. But right now it's us. So give us our due.

Jeff is a good friend of ours and we're sure he wishes us well, just as we wished him well with his book. In fact, the only thing we've ever had against his book is that we don't get paid royalties on it. We only get paid royalties for our books. That practice doesn't seem fair to us, especially since his was a best seller and we have no guarantee how ours is going to go. But this is how publishers do it, so for right now, we have to operate within the system.

Rick and Bubba's Big Honkin' Book of Huntin' was destined to be written. As much as we've talked about the sport of hunting on the Rick and Bubba radio show, it was just a matter of time before hunting experts like us were asked to write a book on the subject. We even brought our guns to the publisher's contract signing ceremony. Looking back on the session, the guns seemed to help things go a little more in our favor. We're thinking about bringing them to all our contract negotiations.

All that to say, what you hold in your hands is the result of years . . . okay, months . . . all right, weeks . . . of hard work to bring you what we hope will truly be the last book you'll ever need on hunting.

So whether you're reading this book in your bed, in your car, in your hunting house, or in the humor aisle of Barnes and Noble, we hope you'll enjoy reading it as much as we enjoyed writing it. And if you are still in Barnes and Noble, the least you could do for us is gather a group together, hand out copies and have a book reading. *(Do we have to tell you everything?!)*

In the meantime, Happy Hunting!

RICK · BUBBA

WHY HUNT?

Why do we do it? Why do grown men (women and kids, too) wake up in what is the middle of the night to most people, dress up like a tree, and go out in the freezing cold to either stand in a hunting house or climb to a tree stand and spend the next several hours hoping and praying that some doe or buck will come out into the clearing? Why do we hunt turkeys, quail, wild boars, and other such animals?

Here are just a few of our own personal reasons:

First, when you're that far out in the wilderness, no one can reach you on your cell phone. That fact alone should have every man in America running to the nearest sporting goods store to suit up. Men, until you've experienced it, you have no idea how precious that "no cell phone" kind of silence can be. No matter how cool your ringtone is, it is even more wonderful not to hear it for an entire day . . . or even longer.

Another reason to go hunting is the fact that baths and showers are optional.

The women may not appreciate this, but kids and most guys think it's great. It's freeing to allow your body the liberty to emit whatever kind of odor it wants to—a freedom experienced by far too few of us Americans these days (and one seemingly enjoyed only by "that guy" who sits down next to us for a ballgame, movie, or ten-hour plane flight).

One more cool thing about hunting is that it gives you the rare feeling that comes from eating something that you hunted for that day. Such satisfaction cannot be experienced by bringing home dinner for your family from the drive-thru (unless you happened to hit a buck rounding the corner). No, grilling what you've just hunted takes a man back to life on the frontier, or perhaps even the caveman days. Only, today, you don't have to worry about a T-Rex showing up and carrying off both you and your kill. You just have to worry about your wife showing up and making you go back home to mow the lawn. (Cavemen didn't know how good they had it).

Never having to talk about where to hang a picture or what color and style of curtains should go in the kitchen of the hunting lodge is another reason why many of us guys like to hunt. Hunters don't worry about such things. To this day, neither one of us can say for certain if the hunting lodge we go to even has curtains. This is information a hunter doesn't need to know, and quite frankly, shouldn't know.

Hunting also helps us do our part to help in the great circle of life. Ever since Adam and Eve were evicted from the Garden of Eden, man has had to live off whatever he could grow on the land and whatever animals he could hunt. So, although places like Kroger and McDonalds have streamlined the whole process, in a sense, hunting helps us keep connected to our ancestor Adam. When we're on a hunt, we know what it feels like to have to go out and find our dinner. During less triumphant outings, we've also experienced the agony and shame that comes from succumbing to temptation and scarfing down that last Nutty Buddy bar—the one the whole hunting party is depending on for survival. But while Adam immediately felt remorse and went and put on some leaves, we were already in camo, so we just licked our fingers.

But we did feel bad.

Another reason why we hunt is that we get to shoot a gun without getting arrested. Usually. (More on that later.) For now, just heed this warning: When hunting, you should always be aiming the rifle toward an *animal*. You are not allowed to just start shooting at anything, like your hunting buddy. Sorry, Dick Cheney. (You can't write a hunting book and not mention the vice-president at least once. Or twice. Or . . . well, read on.)

Hunting also gives you an excuse to play with some really fun toys even after you've passed the forty-years-of-age mark. Neither one of us have ever truly wanted to grow up. We're like Peter Pan, without tights. But hunting lets us continue to play with cool toys like rangefinders and binoculars with in-built cameras, even as we're fast approaching AARP status.

Hunting also lets us drive in the mud. On purpose. And without anyone yelling at us to "Miss the pothole!" As a matter of fact, we actually look for potholes, as that's where the most mud tends to hang out. Women just don't understand this need in a man. The fundamental need to get mud all over your car and shoes and wherever else it happens to splatter. We, of course, don't watch mud wrestling, but if we did, it wouldn't be for the women. It would be for the mud. Mud is fun. We've been told (by an eavesdropping worker at Dairy Queen, no less) that this connection with mud goes back to our childhood. It makes sense. We loved playing in the mud back then, and we still love it today.

But for some reason, as soon as a man says "I do," he is expected to give up this part of himself. He has to wash his hands before dinner and keep some sense of personal hygiene. Through trial and error, we have found that hunting is one of the few activities left where a man can actually cover both himself and his truck with mud and nobody makes him jump in the tub or run his truck through a quick car wash. More often than not, nobody even notices the layer of earth he has encased himself in. And believe us, it feels great!

And finally, one unintended positive by-product of hunting, and another reason why we do it, is the fact that camo can make you look thinner. We didn't realize this was the case, but every time we put on camo, the change is too obvious to miss. Especially if we're standing in front of a tree or bush. A hundred pounds or so just disappears right before your eyes. It's the strangest thing. Instead of looking like two sexy fat guys, the camo makes us look like a couple of giant oaks.

Sexy oaks, of course.

~~TEN~~ ELEVEN WAYS TO GET IN SHAPE FOR A HUNT

1. Practice packing your backpack with food of different shapes and sizes to ensure that on the day of the hunt, you will be able to use the space to its fullest potential. There is no reason to shortchange

yourself of one more sandwich due to underdeveloped packing skills.

2. Practice eating in all sorts of weather (you may have to sit on top of your heating and air-conditioning vents to accomplish this.) Experienced hunters know that freezing weather can render the mouth useless if you haven't tried it a few times prior to the hunt. If the vents don't work, ask your local grocery store manager if you can have a picnic in his walk-in freezer, or take a Big Mac meal with you to the tanning salon. (Eating in front of an oscillating fan is good practice too, for days when the forecast is calling for wind gusts of up to thirty miles an hour. But hang tight to your sandwich. It doesn't take much for a ham and cheese to become airborne.)

3. Load all your gear on your back and practice climbing up a tree over and over until you can successfully make it up without dropping anything. There is nothing worse than getting all the way up

the tree, sitting down and getting yourself situated, only to discover you have dropped half your stuff on an unsuspecting family of squirrels at the bottom. If your lunch was among the scattered objects, chances are you are now watching your boloney-with-mustard being carried up a neighboring tree to what you could swear is a chorus of giggles.

4. Practice answering the call of nature by using various plastic containers. This is so you will be ready when you're in that tree stand or shooting house and you suddenly feel the urge to, well . . . you know. A tree stand is not the place for a novice to first try the plastic container technique. There could be occasions when you might be some twenty feet up in the air. Do you really want to die that way?

5. Put on all your gear and test important gadgets like your range finder, grunt call, binoculars, and camera while they are all hanging around your neck. Work on bringing each one up separately

and using them correctly. Trust us, there is nothing worse than looking through the grunt call to count points or trying to take a picture of the deer with a range finder. Proper use of equipment must be second nature to the hunter, and it has been well documented that an inexperienced hunter could easily strangle himself if these various maneuvers are not rehearsed and mastered.

6. Practice survival techniques for whenever you are dropped off on land that you haven't hunted before, even if everyone assures you that your tree stand will be easy to find. You might want to scout out any bodies of water ahead of time, and it is wise to get used to the taste of bugs. If you've ever found yourself wandering in the darkness for two hours before giving up and just sitting by a tree waiting to be picked up, then you know how important these survival techniques can be. It's also a good idea to make sure that you leave on good terms with the people who drop you off, so they will be more inclined to come back and pick you up.

7. In front of a mirror, practice this saying for the other hunters at the camp: "What? I didn't shoot." Shrug your shoulders like you have no idea where that gunshot came from. And try to look convincing.

8. Practice getting in and out of the back of a truck or ATV, especially if it's been a while since you have done anything athletic. (Watching golf on TV doesn't count).

9. Practice hiding a spike that you just shot when you thought you were shooting a doe. If possible, find a deer of the roadkill variety, put it in the truck, drop it off in your yard and go through your hiding techniques with the young buck. The neighbors might wonder why there are antlers sticking out of your mailbox, but you can just smile and wave, and then walk on back into the house. (As for the other incriminating, uh, evidence pointing to the deer's sex, cross your fingers and hope no one looks).

10. Time how long it takes for you to get your truck packed and backed out of the driveway before your

wife asks you to do something around the house. With daily practice, hunters have been known to shave three or four minutes off of their escape.

11. Practice faking interference on your cell phone for when your wife calls you in front of the other hunters to tell you about her day with the kids. Example: "Honey, I love you . . . you are breaking up . . . bad reception here . . . I can't hear you . . . looks like I'll have to call you later . . ."

RICK · BUBBA

TEN WAYS TO MAKE SURE YOU GET UP WHEN THE ALARM GOES OFF ON HUNTING DAY

1. Sleep in Bubba's room because with Bubba's snoring, chances are you'll still be awake when the alarm goes off.

2. Set the alarm to the music of The Culture Club.

3. Program your alarm to emit the exact sound of bacon cooking (some "smart" models may be able to give off the scent as well).

4. Sleep with the alarm in the pocket of your pajamas

5. Go hunting with Rick, Bubba, Speedy, and all their children. In this setting, no adult can oversleep . . . even if he wanted to.

6. Eat something the night before that was cooked by one of the members of the hunting club.

7. Sleep with one of the hunting dogs.

8. Attach electrodes from the clock to some part of the body (place may vary by the individual).

9. Sleep in the truck that will drop you off at your stand.

10. Use your alarm as a pillow.

IDEAL SNACKS TO PACK FOR A HUNTING TRIP

1. Peanut butter crackers (man's ultimate survival food)

2. M & M's

3. Beef jerky (or old boloney, if unavailable)

4. Butterfinger

5. Snickers

6. Take a Buddy Bar, cut in half with a butter knife, add more peanut butter, then put back together and place in a sandwich bag. (Trust us, you will thank us for this one).

7. Chocolate chip cookies

8. Fudge

9. Porterhouse steak (aged 28-30 days)

10. Cornbread

11. Biscuits

12. Chex Mix

13. Chocolate pretzels

14. Twinkies

15. Four granola bars (to brace rear tires of truck in place)

RICK AND BUBBA'S BUMPER STICKERS FOR THE HUNTER

- White Tail Deer–the original organic free range meat

- Ask me about my Trophy Bucks.

- How's my hunting? Invite me by calling 1-866-WE-BE-BIG

- I am proud of my buck-slaying honor roll student!

- I send my money to Academy Sports and Outdoors.

- Yes, my car is junk, but you should see my ATV.

- I Brake for Trophy Bucks . . . then park, get to a tree, set up, and shoot 'em!

- Help me! My future son-in-law doesn't hunt.

- What does any of this have to do with hunting?

- Life is what happens in between hunts.

Before Bubba and his daughter, Katelyn, go on their hunt, they just have one question: *Who's got the snacks?*

TEN QUALITIES OF THE IDEAL HUNTING PARTNER

He or she:

1. Always says, "You pick your spot first, then I'll pick mine."

2. Always says, "Hey, I love to field dress a deer!"

3. Brings home-cooked snacks from his perfect hunter's wife

4. Always says, "Let's take my truck!"

5. Has access to great hunting land at a moment's notice

6. Better yet, owns his own outstanding hunting land

7. Has beautiful hunting lodge that he never has enough time for and wants you to use

8. Owns a major line of hunting equipment

9. Keeps saying to you, "Hey, go ahead and keep that four-wheeler, I've got plenty."

10. Has the last name Boone or Crockett

Rick and the Killer B's—Brooks "Big Love" and Brody "Taz" Burgess. From Rick's smile you can tell this shot was probably taken before the hunt.

An example of incorrect "field dressing"

RICK AND BUBBA WEATHER REPORTS

"Rain expected throughout the day" means:

You'll be sitting in the lodge hearing every hunter say "Hey, I killed a big one in weather just like this." But not one of them will ever leave the lodge to prove he believes it.

"High winds" means:

You'll be in a shooting house or a tree stand hanging on

for dear life seeing nothing, while the same guy in the example above will be at the lodge still in bed saying to any others who were smart enough to stay behind, "Hey, I killed a nice one in wind just like this."

"Freezing temperatures . . . a low of 12 degrees" means:

Still warm from energetic discussions of "Hey, the deer will move in this weather," you sit at your post, waiting to kill a big one. Then, an hour or so later, as three of your appendages approach frostbite, your grand visions of deer have been replaced by dreams of the fireplace back at the lodge.

"Unseasonably warm" means:

You'll be sweating in full body camo, fighting off bugs, and wondering if you are sitting with a snake.

"Snow" means:

You'll never leave the lodge due to grown men losing the will to hunt due to the sheer joy of an all day snowball fight. (Snow ranks second only to mud.)

THE OFFICIAL RICK AND BUBBA COMPASS

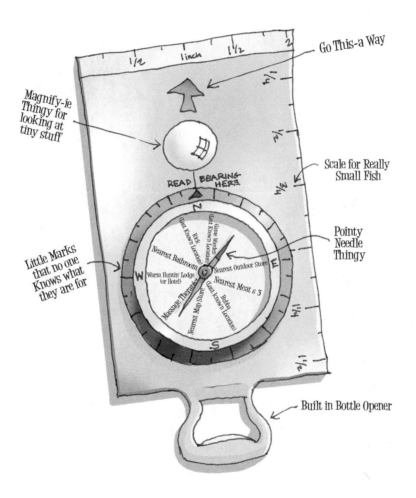

Go This-a Way

Magnify-ie Thingy for looking at tiny stuff

READ BEARING HERE

Scale for Really Small Fish

Pointy Needle Thingy

Little Marks that no one Knows what they are for

Game Warden (Last Known Location)

Rick (Last Known Location)

Nearest Bathroom

Nearest Outdoor Store

Warm Huntin' Lodge (or Hotel)

Nearest Meat & 3

Massage Therapist

Nearest Map Store

Bubba (Last Known Location)

Built in Bottle Opener

The Custom Rick & Bubba Woodsman's Compass

TEN THINGS TO SAY TO YOUR WIFE/ GIRLFRIEND TO CONVINCE HER NOT TO COME ALONG ON YOUR HUNTING TRIP

1. "But, honey, I don't want to put you in danger of being attacked by a rabid bobcat."

2. "I hate to take you away from that day of shopping that I've been wanting you to have. Here's your new credit card."

3. "I'm concerned that camouflage might not be flattering to your figure." (CAUTION: If you use this one, be prepared to duck.)

4. "But, sweetie, if you're with me all weekend you won't be surprised by that jewelry I was going to bring home for you."

5. "How can I miss you if you won't stay here?" (Wasn't that a country song?)

6. "I wanted to tell all the other guys at the hunting camp how wonderful you are, and it just won't be the same with you sitting there."

7. "I don't want the other guys at the camp to feel bad when they realize their wives aren't as pretty as you."

8. "I'm concerned all that outdoor air and overgrown brush will give you dry skin."

9. "I'm sorry, babe, but hunter's orange is just not in your season."

10. "Honey, I have two words for you—no bathroom."

The Rick and Bubba kids . . . ready to hunt.
(If you can't see them, it's the camouflage.)

RICK AND BUBBA'S ROAD SIGNS FOR HUNTERS

Big Buck Crossing

Last Chance for Ammo

Men Hunting Ahead

Yield to oncoming turkeys

Do not pick up hitchhikers in PETA tee shirts

It's 3 AM. Do you know where your hunting license is?

No U-turns in hunting season.

Speed checked by Cheetah

Caution: Falling Snakes

Scenic View Ahead—an 8-point trophy buck and a herd of doe (but you didn't stop for ammo, did you?)

RICK ⬧ BUBBA

TEN WAYS TO CROSS AN OVERFLOWING CREEK TO GET TO YOUR HUNTING HOUSE

1. In memory of the late great Evil Knievel, set up a ramp and jump the creek on your ATV

2. Pole vault using a sturdy tree branch (but we recommend unloading your gun first and strapping it to your back)

3. Drive over it in your four-wheel drive truck. (Come on, you know nothing can stop a truck.)

Blake Burgess wondering why Dad got the *good* hunting house . . . again!

4. Make a canoe out of a fallen tree and cross the creek in it (this is a no-brainer for us Native Americans).

5. Eat your snacks and then blow air in all your empty sandwich bags and use them as floatees.

6. Swing over the creek on a vine. (Hey, it worked for Tarzan, and it worked for you when you had to get out of that tree stand the hard way.)

7. Float over on one of those floating chairs with the drink holder.

8. Jump a ramp with skis while being pulled by a truck to get up to speed. (This requires forethought, for proper equipment).

9. Put your arms over two large Canada geese and let them paddle you across.

10. Float over in an old Volkswagen.

RICK · BUBBA

IN THE DARK

There is no darkness like the darkness one finds after being dropped off at a hunting area as those truck lights pull away and fade into the distance. You're all alone out there. It's just you and the wildlife. And maybe an ax murderer; who knows? You have no idea what is in front of you, behind you, getting ready to crawl up your pant's leg, or drop on you from overhead. All you know is that it's dark and it's scary.

What's more, sounds amplify in the darkness. In the

early darkness, crickets and cicadas can sound like a rock concert. Add on the fact that you've probably seen a scary movie the night before, and your heart will just about beat itself out of your chest.

This brings us to one of our favorite hunting stories. It's a story that was shared with us by a fellow hunter, and friend of the Rick and Bubba Show. We'll try to retell it here as best we can.

It seems this hunter had been driven out to a dark field early one morning for a day of hunting. After being dropped off with all of his gear, he threw his backpack over his shoulder, gathered up the rest of his gear, and began following the guide's directions to the hunting house. It wasn't long before he started getting the feeling that something was following him. He knew it wasn't his wife. She was back at home in bed. He knew it wasn't the guide because he had watched him pull away hours ago; by now, he was long gone. Still, with every step that he took, he could hear slight rustling noises behind him. No matter how hard he tried to talk himself out of it, the feeling that he was being stalked grew stronger and stronger. Each time he stopped the rustling sounds behind him would stop too. When he would start walking again, the sounds would return, perfectly synchronized to his own steps. Whatever it was, a bear, a mountain lion, a rabid boar, or Sasquatch, something was clearly stalking him, waiting for the most opportune time to pounce.

Even when he had to cross a stream, he could hear something breaking through the water behind him. This was one determined beast. It was certain to be a fight to the death, with only one of them surviving. The man hoped and prayed it would be him.

In an attempt to catch the animal off-guard, he waited until he had made it across the creek, then he walked a little farther through the brush, with the blood thirsty critter closing in behind him. There was no more time to waste. Mustering up every ounce of courage inside of him, the man quickly turned around. His plan was to shine the light of his miner's hat directly into the eyes of the beast, or the crazed killer, temporarily blinding him, thus giving the hunter the advantage he needed.

But when the light lit up the darkness behind him, the man, gun in hand and heart in stomach, discovered that it wasn't a wild animal following him at all. The menacing tracker tormenting him for the entire morning had simply been his safety harness dragging behind him!

RICK • BUBBA •

DO YOU HEAR WHAT I HEAR?

As a virtuoso tunes his ear to slight differences in pitch, or a Southern man trains his nose to the different flavors of frying bacon, we serious hunters have learned to distinguish between the various—and often spooky—sounds in the woods. Here's a primer course for any novices out there:

Noise in the Woods	What It Could Be
Gunshot	1. A hunter has just fired and harvested a trophy buck.
	2. Rick's brother Greg missed another deer.
	3. Someone just got a tick off him the hard way.
Eerie wailing	1. An animal is injured; predators may be moving in.
	2. Bubba is snoring in his shooting house.
	3. Hillary Clinton is making a speech near your spot.
Crunching of Leaves and the Breaking of Twigs	1. A trophy buck is making his way toward you.
	2. The game warden is about to ask for your license.
	3. Rick is eating tortilla chips with salsa.

Noise in the Woods	What It Could Be
Roar of an Animal	1. A bobcat or cougar is near.
	2. Speedy's body is responding to last night's Mexican fiesta theme at the hunting lodge.
	3. The Big Foot legend is going to be solved once and for all.
Blood Curdling Scream	1. Don Juan lost his flash light.
	2. Someone has just found a snake in their backpack.
	3. Bubba's roommate just found out Bubba did not bring his CPAP mask.
Engine Running	1. Your guide has placed you near a busy railroad.
	2. A farmer has chosen now to till the garden.
	3. Bubba is lost on his four-wheeler again.

Noise in the Woods	What It Could Be
Large Bird of Flight Flapping its Wings	1. Turkeys are leaving their roost.
	2. A screech owl is hunting near you.
	3. Don Juan is hanging upside down in his safety harness, flapping his arms. (*You think we're kidding.*)
Water Running	1. You are near a relaxing babbling brook.
	2. The cooler the kids got you for Father's Day is leaking.
	3. Someone has finally answered the call of two bottled waters, one Coca-Cola and a giant Powerade.

Noise in the Woods

Screech of Tires

What It Could Be

1. Someone in the hunting party is stuck in the mud.

2. Someone in the hunting party is reliving their burn-out days from high school.

3. In the solitude and beauty of the great outdoors, someone just remembered it's his anniversary.

TEN SIGNS YOU'RE IN A GOOD HUNTING SPOT

1. A taxidermist gives you his card as you head to your stand.

2. Does keep pointing to the woods.

3. There's a sign in the middle of the food plot that reads (in hoof prints): "Gone to bed, be back around 3 pm. Meet me then."

4. Police are called to remove the hunter that was in the stand the day before but couldn't pull himself away.

5. Coyotes ask you, "Can we have whatever you don't want?"

6. You are afraid to rattle due to the fear that one of the eight bucks you're looking at will take you up on the challenge.

7. A buck walks into the food plot with a sign on his back that reads "Don't shoot! More to come."

8. Ted Nugent is already there.

9. When your hunting spot is announced, the other hunters throw their hats down.

10. PETA protesters hoisting signs try to block your path to the spot.

RICK • BUBBA

TEN SIGNS YOU'RE IN A BAD HUNTING SPOT

1. When you arrive, thousands of people are standing in the green field. A band is playing, and a football whizzes by.

2. When you arrive, the game warden is already there and says he has nothing else to do, so he'll be sitting with you for the rest of the day.

3. You can order breakfast from the fast food restaurant that's 100 yards from where you're sitting.

4. Small children walk under your stand to get their dog to go back into the house.

5. The guide points out your tree stand, and the other hunters begin to giggle.

6. It's hard to hear the movement of any game over the sounds of the train rolling down the tracks.

7. Prior to going out you receive a letter from PETA that says they're perfectly fine with you hunting in that area.

8. A starving coyote is the only animal you see.

9. As you lumber up the tree to your spot, you can't help feeling like surrounding squirrels are shaking their heads in pity.

10. The tree is graffitied with hour-marks and mournful sonnets penned by previous hunters.

Perfect spot, Bubba!

ALTERNATIVE WAYS TO CLIMB TO A TREE STAND IF THE LADDER IS BROKEN

- Trampoline

- Swing from a vine hanging from a nearby tree (loin cloth not advised, but Tarzan yell is optional)

- Get chased by a hungry bear

- Learn to walk in stilts and then just walk over to it and sit down

- Get bitten by a radioactive spider with huge fangs

- Have one of those acrobatic teams from China build a human ladder

- Have a friend shoot you out of a silent cannon

- Parachute in, land in the top of the tree, and then climb down to the stand

- Rent a giraffe

- Two words (or is it one?): Pole Vault

TEN WAYS TO GET DEER TO COME OUT INTO THE OPEN

1. Come back the day after hunting season is over. They will be everywhere.

2. Build a paved road right through the middle of the food plot. They will be everywhere.

3. Put a guy in the stand who has never hunted a day of his life. They will be everywhere . . .until you pick up your gun.

4. Roll around in raw corn before you get in your stand.

5. Dress like a beautiful doe (CAUTION: if your buddy misses the shot, you'd better know how to run!)

6. Put up a sign that says, "Stand here to be on TV."

7. Forget to load your gun.

8. Fall asleep.

9. Forget to sight your gun.

10. Pull up in your driveway and let your headlights hit the front yard after you have been hunting for 14 hours, 350 miles from home and haven't seen a thing all day. They will be everywhere.

HOW TO TELL THE DIFFERENCE BETWEEN QUAIL AND AN ENDANGERED WINGED SPECIES

You might think this list is "for the birds," but it might mean the difference between a fowl meal with surrounding friends and a foul kill with pursuing law enforcement.

1. Quail do not have deadly talons.

2. Quail aren't big enough to be flying by with a trout in their beak.

3. Dogs rarely if ever point to eagles or hawks.

4. Quail don't sit on cliffs.

5. Quail don't look a lot like our national symbol.

6. Both Bob White and the bald eagle have white on their heads; quail don't.

7. Never has a quail been seen with a six-foot wing-span.

8. A quail is usually bigger than its eggs.

9. No one has ever seen a covey of condors.

10. Quail rarely fly into a stadium during the national anthem.

RICK AND BUBBA'S EMERGENCY SIGNALS

The following may be employed as text messages or 2-way radio messages to enable you to get help in emergency situations without causing a panic:

"Is it 'if red touches yellow it will kill a fellow?'
Just wondering."

"Eware-bay the obcat-bay!"

"Are squirrels usually rabid?"

"Can bears climb pine trees?"

"Has anyone seen my hunting license?"

"Who's the guy with the slingblade?"

"Does anyone know for certain where the property line is?"

"I just saw Burt Reynolds and Ned Batey."

"Do raccoons bite? And how tall do they usually grow?"

"Do deer typically have brands on them?"

RICK AND BUBBA'S BINOCULAR-FREE VIEWING CHART

Without binoculars, it's not always easy to correctly guess what that shadowy figure is starring at you from across the field. That is why we are providing the *Rick and Bubba's Binocular-Free Chart* to help you determine what it is you're actually seeing when you think you're seeing something else.

What You Think You See	What It Really Is
Bigfoot	Bubba with no shirt on
Smokey the Bear	A state trooper
A 12-point Buck	A spike with his head in some branches
A Really Big Doe	A cow
A Coyote	Someone's dog down the road
25-pound Gobbler	2-pound chicken
Black Panther	Abandoned black cat
Elk	Kudzoo
Your Hunting Buddy	The game warden
Someone Walking	Your wife through the food plot

TEN WAYS TO GET THE BEST THANKSGIVING TURKEY IN YOUR SIGHTS

1. Be deer hunting when it's not turkey season.

2. Visit a zoo.

3. Hunt in the middle of the day after all the "experts" told you turkeys will only come to you in the morning.

4. Take someone with you that has never killed a turkey and isn't even wearing camo.

5. Look for that one turkey who isn't spooked by noise and movement. That's right. The one your hunting buddy already shot.

6. Rent the guy who is always on late night talks shows doing turkey calls.

7. Fly the Macy's Thanksgiving parade turkey balloon over an open field.

8. Find where all those Butterball turkeys come from and hunt there.

9. Realize you brought you son's BB gun instead of your shotgun and make do.

10. Have your son practice shooting cans, and then when the last shell is used and you're just about to go home, turn around and look . . . the

    perfect turkey will be standing there

RICK • BUBBA

TEN SUREFIRE WAYS TO GET YOUR PICTURE IN OUTDOOR SPORTS MAGAZINES

Bubba and Katelyn hot on the trail of a Pizza Hut.

1. Kill a doe that has horns.

2. Shoot Big Foot.

3. Catch the Loch Ness Monster.

4. Accidentally shoot Dick Cheney with birdshot on a hunting trip

5. Wrestle a deer and kill it with a spoon.

6. Be saved from the mouth of a catfish the size of a Volkswagen.

7. Wear a loin cloth and hunt with a spear.

8. Invent a bigger ATV.

9. Start a new line of camo that features a shooting house pattern.

10. Get lost, and then be taken in by a nice family of coyotes who raise you until you're taken in by a carefree bear named Baloo.

THINGS TO DO IN THE HUNTING HOUSE WHILE WAITING FOR BUCK TO APPEAR

1. Finish your taxes.

2. Coordinate your kid's Little League schedule with the upcoming turkey season.

3. Watch movies on your iPhone.

4. Break off little twigs and thump field goals inside the shooting house.

5. Write out that romantic poem for your wife that springs to your mind whenever you see her or hear her name (come on, guys, my wife may read this book).

6. Take your range finder and try to figure out how far away every single tree is that you can see.

7. Change your phone company.

8. See if you can get the sunlight to burn an ant through your binoculars.

9. Take a nap and watch for deer at the same time. (Hint: This technique is very similar to taking a nap and watching television at the same time, or napping while driving.)

10. Watch your hopes dwindle from a trophy buck to a cull buck to a doe, and finally, to any squirrel that crosses your path.

11. Read the entire Rick and Bubba catalog of books.

12. Recap over and over the final conversation you had with your wife before you left and what you should have said had you thought of it at the time.

13. Start anticipating whatever hunt is after this one and convince yourself the deer will move for you then.

14. Decide against saying any of those things that you think you should have said in that final conversation with your wife before leaving on your hunting trip.

RICK · BUBBA·

SOMETIMES IT'S JUST NOT MEANT TO BE

Greg "Haystacks" Stewart was my (Rick) college room-mate when we both played football at Troy State University in South Alabama. He's a great friend and he loves to duck hunt.

God has blessed 'Stacks with four beautiful daughters,

but no sons. We believe that God is getting even with 'Stacks. Let us explain. For a man who stands six-feet-tall, and weighs three hundred pounds and is all about the outdoors, it's been hard on him to not have any boys to take hunting with him. Not that girls don't hunt. They do. Our daughters love it. But when 'Stacks decided one day to take some of his

Bubba and son, Hunter, wonder who ate the last Nutty Buddy bar.

daughters duck hunting with him, things didn't turn out quite as planned. The day went okay up to the point where he had finally gotten everyone settled in the duck blind. The girls were keeping their voices down and enjoying a nice breakfast when one precious daughter asked Daddy what was going to happen. 'Stacks explained (naively, we think) that as soon as the ducks swooped down into the water to land, he would stand up out of the blind and shoot at them with his shotgun.

The moment finally came and the ducks were coming in for a landing. The timing couldn't have been more perfect. But just when he was about to stand up and shoot the ducks, his daughters stood up and started waving their hands, screaming "Fly away! Fly away! My dad is going to shoot you!!!"

Needless to say, the ducks listened. We understand he has since made his daughters members of Ducks Unlimited . . . but shhh . . . don't say anything.

YOU PROBABLY MISSED THE DEER IF . . .

1. The buck is headed back into the woods singing "Missed me, missed me, now you have to kiss me . . ."

2. A tree falls.

3. The deer keeps eating.

Don't spook him, Bubba!

Katelyn and J.C. count Rick and Bubba's misses.

4. You have been walking around in the dark woods for four hours, haven't seen the first sign of any kill, and you took the shot at 7 a.m.

5. After your shot, you then hear another shot from the field several hundred yards behind you (and it's in the direction that the deer happened to be running).

6. Your scope still had the cap on it.

7. You shot at it at 400 yards with a shotgun.

8. After you put your gun down, you look through your binoculars and see deer laughing.

9. Immediately following your shot, your guide says "OK, let's move to the truck and try somewhere else."

10. You bought your first gun on the way to the hunt.

RICK · BUBBA

TEN THINGS YOU SAY WHEN YOU MISS A SHOT

1. "It's okay. I usually shoot over their heads and scare them to death so as not to ruin the meat."

2. "Just as I was about to shoot I remembered that I forgot to take the trash out to the road."

3. "I don't know what happened. I just couldn't get that *Bambi* film out of my mind."

4. "One of my kids was sitting with me and grabbed the binoculars around my neck just as I was about to shoot."

5. "I couldn't concentrate, honey, because I kept thinking about how much I missed you."

6. "I was trying to let my son shoot. See what happens when you do something nice?"

7. "I guess when I dropped my gun after being attacked by that bear, my scope fell off."

8. "I was aiming at that tree. Really."

9. "I know I hit him; we just couldn't find where he dropped."

10. "Shoot? I didn't shoot. That was a backfire. Or Speedy and the Mexican food again."

WHAT A DEER THINKS WHEN A SHOT MISSES HIM

- Wow! That was a loud noise! . . . But what does that have to do with that very attractive doe over there?

- Phew! That fly that just whizzed by me must be taking growth hormones.

- Why do I have the sudden urge to take off running? I have got to switch to decaf!

- I told you this guy couldn't hit the side of a barn.

- Hey, I'm trying to eat here!

- *What was I thinking?!* Feed at night, you idiot!

- I haven't been this scared since the Blue Tongue Panic of '01!

- I knew I shouldn't have eaten the spicy acorns.

- Note to self: If large primate is wearing clothes that seem to clash, don't walk into the open.

- Okay, my turn now!

RICK · BUBBA ·

WE'VE GOT FEELINGS, TOO

Why is it when you bring your son or daughter with you on a hunting trip, or even your wife, the guide and everyone else in the group will try their best to put them on a deer? Don't get us wrong, we think it's great that they want to make sure our loved ones don't go home empty-handed.

But what about *us*? We don't want to go home empty-handed either!

Rick with his oldest son, Blake "Boomer" Burgess, and Dan Moultrie.
Blake shot this big buck that day. They wouldn't let me hunt.
I could only watch. Notice my fake smile.

Oh, we try to look excited for our offspring and cheer on our sweetheart as the guide helps them line up that 8-point buck in their sights. And if we happen to trip and make them lose their aim or spontaneously yell out "Earthquake!," it was merely an accident. We would never intentionally interfere with their shot.

Rick tries bribing deer with autographed hat.

RICK · BUBBA

HOW TO KNOW WHEN A STORM IS SEVERE ENOUGH TO PACK UP YOUR HUNTING GEAR AND CALL IT A DAY

1. When you wake up from your nap, the shooting house has moved and landed on top of a dead witch.

2. Deer are flying past your window, and they are not pulling a sleigh.

3. All over the woods, animals are grabbing a date and loading onto some funny looking boat.

4. Raccoons come by your hunting house and ask, "Hey, got any room in there?"

5. You consider putting down the gun and going fishing instead . . . from your tree stand.

6. You see fish swimming beside you . . . *inside your boat.*

7. FEMA trailers are being set up in your green field.

8. People run into your blind screaming, "Is this a storm shelter?!"

9. Your ATV starts itself and tries to leave.

10. Your hunting dogs load themselves into the truck . . . *in the driver's seat*

RICK · BUBBA

"YOU'RE ALL UNDER ARREST"

I (Rick) am probably the one to blame for infecting the entire radio station with the hunting bug. Some of us hunted with our dads when we were younger, but it had been years since we had donned camouflage and taken to the woods. But one day I got to talking to the guys and before we knew it, we had accepted an invitation to go to Alabama and do a live radio show during an actual hunt. A fan had been kind enough to offer his land for the hunt and since the price was right (free), we took him up on it.

Now before I go on, I should tell you a few of the factors that we were up against that day. Number one, the weather wasn't good for a hunt. It was hot. We're talking Alabama hot. It doesn't get much hotter than Alabama hot. If you dumped a trainload of ice in hell, it might run a close second. (That's a slight exaggeration, of course. But only slight.) Also, because of the heat, the fields were dry and mostly dirt. There was hardly a grassy patch in sight. And lastly, it had been years since any of us had hunted, so we were all a little sketchy about the rules.

As you can see, it was clearly a recipe for disaster.

Bubba's disaster came first. He got lost trying to find his tree. Forget the fact that he had wisely scouted out the location the day before because any hunter knows everything looks different in the pitch blackness of those early morning hours: It hadn't helped him. He still couldn't find his spot. And while he was driving all over the field, the rest of us were trying to find our locations, too.

Finally, Bubba spotted his tree stand, parked the car, got

his gear and climbed up into the tree. As soon as he got situated, he started to doze off (there's something about a tree stand that works better than any sleeping pill on the market). That's about when he heard someone on the ground trying to get his attention. At first he wondered if it was a deer, but then he saw the badge. (Most deer don't wear badges.)

"Hey!" the voice in the darkness called up to him again. "You know you're hunting in a baited field?"

Bubba was wide-awake now. He recognized the uniform as that of a game warden. Baited field? What was the game warden talking about?

"No," Bubba said, as innocently as possible.

"Do you see those green things over there?" the warden pointed off into the distance to some grassy patches, those "hardly a grassy patch in sight" patches. It turns out they were alfalfa cubes. Deer love alfalfa, and you're lot allowed to put it out there in order to bait the deer. Hence the term "baited field." But Bubba didn't know any of this. All he knew was there was a game warden at the bottom of his tree stand, and he didn't look very happy.

Meanwhile, I was at another location on the land, unaware

that Bubba and the rest of the radio station crew were being arrested for hunting on a baited field—all while we were live on the air. My brother, Greg, almost got us all into even more trouble when the warden asked him if he knew what the green patches of alfalfa were for.

"No," Greg said, "but the deer seem to like it, so leave it alone."

Apparently, that wasn't the right answer.

While everyone was being rounded up and the day was slipping away, I was still out there in the woods all alone wondering why no one was coming back to pick me up. All sorts of possible scenarios were running through my brain . . . bear attack, aliens, the Rapture, my buddies being mobbed by our adoring fans. Not once had the thought of a mass arrest crossed my mind. I climbed down out of my tree stand and started walking, passing empty tree stand after empty tree stand. What had happened to everybody? These were stands that should have had our people in them, but now their doors were just blowing in the wind. As I neared our lodge, someone managed to break away from the warden long enough to drive out and pick me up and fill me in on the unfortunate turn of events.

After a lot of explaining and our invitation to the warden to stay and eat with us (no, not venison), we finally seemed to get the situation resolved. None of us had knowingly done anything wrong, but we still vowed never to do it again.

But then, after dinner, the warden decided that since we were all gathered together there, he might as well check our hunting permits. For most of us this wasn't a problem. However, for a few in our party, it just wasn't their day.

So that's the story of our first group hunting expedition. We weren't taken in, but we got cited by the warden and it was all aired live. We billed it as sort of our "What not to do during hunting season" show, and it became one of our most requested reruns. They may even show it annually at the Game Wardens Convention.

RICK   BUBBA

TEN + ONE THINGS TO SAY TO A GAME WARDEN

1. "Has anyone ever told you that green is your color?

2. "Man, I am glad you are here. I was just sitting in my tree stand thinking of how much money I wanted to donate to the Fish and Game Department."

3. "Have I ever shown you pictures of all my children and wife who depend on me for their daily needs?"

4. "Would you mind sitting with me in this shooting house? I just need someone to talk to."

5. "Hey, I've got good news! I just saw a bear with a picnic basket and he went that way!"

6. "Are you guys sort of like state troopers without the pavement?"

7. "Say, who was your favorite Beatle?"

8. "Is a platypus a mammal?"

9. "Don't you think all these species of ducks get a little confusing?"

10. "Hey, looks like I shot the horns off of this one."

11. "I don't know what that stuff is, but the deer sure seem to love it."

RICK · · BUBBA ·

OOPS!

Anyone who has watched Tom Wilcox's outdoors television show knows that he is a former NFL player from Cajun country, and one great hunter. But Bubba and I (Rick) had been a guest on his show four or five times and had never taken a deer. The situation was getting embarrassing, and we were becoming the butt of a whole string of jokes. We also knew that there had to be some kind of jinx, and we were desperate to break it. We weren't exactly sure which one in our party was causing the jinx, but since Tommy

"But they looked so much bigger from a distance."

doesn't seem to have any trouble bagging a deer on his own, Bubba and I were the prime suspects.

Before we go on, for any of you less experienced hunters, I need to point out that the standards of deer hunting are that you don't shoot a buck that's less than 8-points. They will, however, let you take a doe because they say it helps with the management of the deer population.

Once again, Tommy called and lined us up for a hunting trip. Expectations that the jinx would be thwarted and Bubba and I would go home with a trophy buck, or at the very least a doe, were running high.

On the day of the hunt Bubba, my nephew, my brother, three of my sons, Bubba's daughter Katelyn, and I all loaded into the vehicles and headed out to the hunting field. Our chances looked promising as soon as we got there. A bunch of does showed up, and we knew that with all those ladies around, it wouldn't be long before a bachelor came cruising by. Sure enough, he did. One showed up and ran out into the field, forgetting everything his father taught him because of those beautiful does.

I reached for my hunting rifle. But about that time that

deer's brains must have kicked back in because he took off leaping through the woods, no doubt intent on checking out a safer singles gathering.

"Why didn't you shoot at it?" Tommy asked.

I didn't want to get into the whole jinx thing again, but I do think that had a lot to do with the way things turned out. That, and the fact that I couldn't get my gun sighted in time. Disappointed in myself now, and even more determined than ever not to come home empty handed, I followed Tommy and the others down toward another hunting spot. I'm not sure how far we had to walk, but after we had hiked through the tall brush, we finally turned left, and saw one of the most beautiful open fields I had ever seen. And what made it even more spectacular was the fact that there was a doe running through it right out in the open.

I did the only thing a man in my situation, and on camera for one of the most popular hunting shows on television (did I mention I had never taken a deer yet on his show?) could do. I fired one shot and put that doe on the ground. I couldn't believe it! I was so excited I could hardly stand it. I had just bagged a beautiful doe, and it was all documented

Rick and Bubba's Hunting Tip #136: "Never hunt without plenty of witnesses."

on film for the whole world to see. (I'm making a mental note to myself to be sure this footage makes it to my Biography special . . . whenever they call.)

About this time, Tommy (with what I sensed as more than a hint of jealousy in his voice) said, "Come on, Rick, let's go over and take a look at what you got."

Good call, Tommy, I thought to myself. Of course we needed to get closer, for the cameras. The crew probably needed to get shots of me with the doe, Tommy with me and the doe, and maybe even do a quick interview with Tommy asking me questions as I stand next to the doe. This was clearly one of my finest moments in hunting. The jinx was finally broken.

With anticipation and adrenaline coursing through my

veins, I and the others walked over to where the doe had fallen. I was even practicing my smile for the camera.

But then . . .

I'm not sure in what exact order we arrived at the doe. All I remember is that when I got there, I was greeted by a deafening silence and a circle of mouths hanging open in disbelief and horror. No cheers joined my own, no high fives, and no offers to hoist me up on shoulders and carry me back to camp. They were all too busy staring at the poor young buck with two little spikes that I had just taken down.

And it was all caught on film.

As soon as I realized what I had done, my own cheering stopped. I immediately tried to do some damage control by putting a positive spin on the situation, asking the others if they, too, had heard about the reports of rabid deer in the area. But no one was buying my spin.

My youngest son put it all in perspective. "Dad, you shot Bambi." I'm sure he didn't mean to have disgust in his voice when he said it. It just came out that way.

Back at the lodge, word spread rather quickly about the unfortunate incident. Some of them could barely bring themselves to look at the video footage of me when I first realized I had killed a young buck. They could barely bring themselves to look at it over and over and over again each time they replayed it. Needless to say, I won a unanimous vote for my induction into the Hunting Camp's Hall of Shame. I felt terrible.

I also felt pretty full because that young buck ate about as good as any venison I'd ever tasted! When you factor in the hunting fine and the cost to my dignity, it came out to about $600 a pound. But the jinx was broken!

I am, however, having second thoughts about including it on my Biography special.

TEN WAYS TO NOTIFY YOUR RIDE THAT YOU'RE READY TO BE PICKED UP

1. Shoot twice, then say into your 2-way radio, "Uh oh."

2. Run through the nearest dirt road or path screaming, "SOMEBODY COME GET ME!"

3. Launch a cloud of colorful helium balloons.

4. Shoot up a flare.

5. Start a fire and send smoke signals.

6. Talk CB jargon in the 2-way radio: "Uhhh . . . Breaker 19, can someone come get the Ridge Runner and take him back to the camp? NOW!"

7. Keep doing the Tarzan yell as loud as you can until your ride gets the message.

8. Start your own fireworks show.

9. Launch a kite made of hunter's orange.

10. Keep text messaging the following: "SOMEBODY COME HELP ME! THERE ARE TOO MANY DEER HERE TO COUNT!!"

RICK AND BUBBA'S IDEAL HUNTING GEAR

1. Two-way radios that actually work and let you really talk to other hunters and hear each other in all kinds of terrain and weather. And they would also play video games.

2. Rick and Bubba hunting boots that fit like athletic shoes but are waterproof and scent-proof. That way, you can play basketball and hunt in the same day. And possibly outrun a coyote.

3. Rick and Bubba binoculars. These will not only show you close-ups of the deer, but you can watch your favorite movies on them. And even when you're otherwise engaged (napping comes to mind), the binoculars will always be watching. You can set them down and they will constantly monitor the field, vibrating whenever something walks into the frame. They'll actually sound an alarm if the "something" is twice your size and breathing on you (bears, for example). The binoculars will also have a GPS, a cell phone, alarm clock, DVD player, and an attached Swiss army knife. No hunter is fully equipped without them.

4. The Rick and Bubba hunting rifle. Our rifle will come complete with a Rick and Bubba video camera that will operate simultaneously with the aim

and firing, capturing it all on digital. The scope/camera lens will capture every hit and every miss. If it's a hit, it will also send the video to your family and friends, along with a text message to your wife saying you'll be home late for dinner. If it's a miss, it will only send the video to your therapist. *Caution:* The gun should only be used to capture a video of the deer and the hunt, not the group shot. Pointing the gun in the direction of your fellow hunters might create a Dick Cheney moment, in which case the video will only be sent to America's Funniest Home Videos, YouTube, and your attorney.

5. Rick and Bubba's Hunter's Orange will actually taste like an orange Dreamsicle. Whether it's your hat, vest, or backpack, all you have to do is lick it and you'll instantly taste ice cream. Why hasn't anyone thought of this before?

6. While we're on the subject, why do they have us wearing camouflage if we're going to also wear that bright orange color, too? Does that make sense to

anyone? They say a deer is color blind, so if that is the case, why are we all dressing up like trees? Wouldn't the colors look the same to them? Even the orange? It doesn't make sense, but we do like the idea of Dreamsicle-flavored clothing.

In fact, we might branch out and make a whole food-flavored wardrobe.

There could be the Rick and Bubba tuxedo that tastes exactly like Oreo cookies. You've already got the black and white thing going, so it just makes sense. Imagine, no more nervous twitching during boring formal affairs. Just suck on your lapel for a few minutes, or give your bowtie a quick lick, and all's right with the world again.

Hot fudge-flavored sweats is another idea whose time has come. If you're going to work out, why not put that elevated body heat to good use and warm up your hot fudge-flavored sweats? It will be a calorie-free treat—sort of like flavored gum. The only danger would be if you actually bite off a chunk of the fabric. You might choke, but hey, no gained weight, so you're cool.

Being from the South, one of our favorites would be the sweet tea flavored t-shirt. We've never understood why they're called *t*-shirts anyway. At least this would give their name some legitimacy.

The Rick and Bubba hot dog-flavored baseball cap seems like a natural to us. Imagine being able to get that great taste of a ballpark hot dog whenever you want by just taking a lick on your baseball cap. Can life get any better? Even the most determined baseball cap wearer would gladly remove his cap if he knew the taste of a sizzling frankfurter awaited him.

And we all know how most men don't like to wear ties, but that would surely change if someone were to buy them the Rick and Bubba Krispy Kreme-flavored tie. Imagine sitting in church waiting for the preacher to get to his last and final "In closing," and all you have to do to temporarily calm those hunger pangs is make one indiscreet swipe of your tie across your tongue. The pastor might even want a tie for himself. (Though this could have the adverse affect of making his sermons longer. But with your own Krispy Kreme flavored neckwear to suck on, what do you care?)

The biggest hit of the entire Rick and Bubble food-flavored clothing line would have to be the Rick and Bubba T-Bone Turtleneck. The close proximity of the turtleneck to the mouth is the primary reason for this brainchild. It's easy to just hang your tongue out and take a lick. Most people probably won't even notice you doing it, especially if it's a red turtleneck.

Note: For those who would rather not suck on their clothes, our line of Rick and Bubba scent-free clothing will be perfect for you. This line is revolutionary in that it will actually *absorb* any scents that your own body might be emitting. It will also neutralize the odor of your four-course breakfast, and in its place exude only the scent of corn. You can eat anything you want—bacon, ham, sausage gravy, anything, and all you'll smell like is corn. You'll smell like the entire state of Iowa. You'll be like a walking corn stalk that just came and sat down in the woods. We realize you can't use corn scent for hunting in a lot of states, but that's the beauty of our clothing line. If a fish and game warden is within fifty yards (it has sensors to pick up their scent, too), the clothing will automatically change the scent back to bacon.) In other words, you could eat anything you want and still hunt without worrying that your body odor is affecting the deer in the least. You can even fry up breakfast right there in the shooting house (with proper ventilation of course), and it won't affect your hunt. The corn smell of your clothes will be so strong it will overpower even the strongest breakfast smells.

Another positive aspect of both our scent-free and our food-flavored clothing line is that you can sleep in our clothes. They're soft, like pajamas.

You don't have to get up and dress while it's still dark. You just wake up and go straight to the car. After your bacon breakfast, of course.

7. Lastly, we recommend the Rick and Bubba's Range Finder. Not only will it tell you how far the trees are, it will also tell you how far away the nearest fast food restaurant is (in case you want more than your clothes to chew on), and help you find the truck keys you dropped in the woods somewhere.

RICK • BUBBA

TEN WAYS TO TELL IF YOU HAVE A TICK ON YOU

1. You hear a slurping sound and no one around you is drinking anything.

2. You don't remember having a mole on your cheek the size of a kumquat *before* the hunting trip.

3. People are chasing you with torches and tweezers.

Coach Burgess and Hunter Bussey . . . Is that Big Foot in the background?

4. You feel the blood being sucked out of you and it's not April 15th.

5. "Hey, look. I've got a new mole."

6. Your wife is checking your hair like a monkey (the upside of this is that it will bring you closer together).

7. You're picking at every mole on your body to see if it has legs.

8. Something the size of a catcher's mask is sucking on your face.

9. Your blood count suddenly drops to negative 4.

10. You feel your backpack pressing against your back. Then you remember you're not wearing a backpack.

Hunter Bussey proves he has mastered the Rick and Bubba Hunting Technique.

RICK · BUBBA

THE PEANUT BUTTER ADVANTAGE

My (Bubba) cousin is an expert in deer behavior. He didn't get his master's degree in it, but he's an expert on the subject just the same. You'll see what I mean by the time you finish reading this chapter.

Now any hunter knows that the biggest part of deer hunting is getting the deer to come out to where you are. Since that's the case, you would think all you'd need to do is put out some deer food and deer would show up like relatives after a lottery win. But that's baiting the deer, and it's not allowed.

But my cousin has figured out a way to stay one step ahead of the game warden, and it's all perfectly legal. You see, he's figured out that deer love peanut butter. I'm not sure how he figured that out, but he did.

Whenever it's not hunting season, he takes the lid off a full plastic container of peanut butter and nails it to a tree. He then cuts off the bottom of the container and screws the jar back into the lid. Basically, what he ends up with is a peanut butter sucker sticking out the side of a tree, which apparently deer love. The deer come up and lick the peanut butter like a Tootsie Roll Pop. When they're finished with that jar, he takes it down and screws on another one. He only does this during the off-season, of course, because once hunting season officially starts, you're not allowed to bait the field. So although he doesn't bait the field, what he has done is give the deer an insatiable taste for peanut butter.

Now all he has to do is sit in his hunting house, open his lunch sack and eat a peanut butter sandwich. It seems harmless enough, but all he has to do is belch or have some other bodily eruption, and the deer come running. According to him, it's legal. And it works! And so far, no deer has gotten his tongue permanently stuck to the roof of his mouth.

RICK AND BUBBA'S CREATIVE WAYS TO TRANSPORT YOUR KILL

We realize that most hunters will be driving their trucks or other four-wheel drive vehicles whenever they go hunting. But sometimes circumstances call for a hunter to depend on alternative forms of transportation. In situations such as these, we figured it is our civic duty to provide you with a few tips for getting your kill home in the following types of vehicles:

Motorcycle—Set the deer on the back like a passenger. Wrap the hoofs around you. If it's small, please put a helmet on it (the antlers might stick out, but do the best you can). Leather pants are optional.

Compact car with luggage rack—We suggest you use the luggage rack for the deer. If you try to stuff it in the trunk, its legs will probably be sticking out and prompt law enforcement to pull you over and ask questions. The luggage rack is the best. Display the deer right out in the open. If hunting in December, you might like to attach a small Santa behind it, as if he's pulling a sleigh.

Small car, no luggage rack—Position deer as if he's a front seat passenger. Then you can drive in the car pool lane. If it's a summer day, open the sunroof so there's more room for the antlers.

Sportscar—Again position deer next to you in the front seat, only put sunglasses on him. If it's a buck, apply hair gel. If it's a doe, lipstick and a nice trendy scarf should work.

Minivan—A hunter having to drive a minivan is embarrassing enough, so you may need to overcompensate for the vehicle and go "old school" when transporting your kill. Try tying the big buck on the hood of the van to prove to everyone you pass that you were able to harvest a deer, even if you are driving a minivan. Besides, it's demeaning to make a deer lie in the back of a minivan amidst a pile of soccer balls and pom-poms.

Bus—Those of you who use only public transportation shouldn't let that stop you from hunting. Just dress your deer up like another bus passenger and step on board. Think of it as *Weekend at Bambi's*. If that seems farfetched, consider dressing your deer up like a hoodlum so everyone would leave him alone. Frankly, if it's a subway, no one will notice anyway.

RICK AND BUBBA'S TIPS ON WHERE TO HANG YOUR TROPHY KILL

1. Wherever your wife tells you to.

    (Off the record, deer must be displayed where your friends can see it and ask you about it. It's the law—really. And it must be hung in a prominent place, like wherever you hung your wedding pictures. Just move them over to the right a little to accommodate the deer head. Right in the middle of your family pictures is also a nice setting for your deer head. For a nice complement to your trophy, try hanging a plaque that reads, "Ask me about this deer.")

What...?

. . . AND WHERE *NOT* TO DISPLAY IT

- Over the toilet; it's not the time or place for that
- On the door of your office at work
- The baby's room
- Over the bed in your master bedroom
- The kitchen, especially on the refrigerator

We recommend against displaying it in your dining room. It's a little weird to be munching on venison while you're looking at a deer head. We don't do that with any other animal that we eat (with the exception of Hawaiian luaus and the whole pig-with-an-apple-in-its-mouth, but that's rare). No, upon reflection we've decided that it's just in bad taste to have your trophy buck looking down on you while you eat his friends.

And finally, don't place horns on the front grill of your car (especially if you tend to tailgate).

HOLD THAT LOOK

When displaying a trophy kill, you want your deer to look rugged. If it looks rugged, that means it was a challenge and you are a skilled sportsman. There is little glory in hanging a deer with any of the following looks:

Surprise

Old and sickly

A red nose

A tag around its neck that says "Bambi"

Rope burn around its neck

No wildlife tag in its ear

Tongue sticking out and both hoofs up by its ears

A silly grin

A monogrammed scarf from its mother

Oh, him? . . . I bagged him in Paris.

RICK · BUBBA·

HOW TO TELL THE DIFFERENCE BETWEEN ROADKILL AND A TROPHY BUCK

In the world of competitive hunting, some unsuccessful hunters employ desperate measures to prove that they, too, can bring a big buck home. Here are some tips to help you spot any trophy buck impersonators.

- Most trophy bucks do not have tire marks.
- Most trophy bucks come with an entire body.
- Most hunters who just took a trophy would not have time to put a suit on for the picture.
- Most hunters who took a trophy would not be driving a rental car.
- There are a lot of high-powered rifles, but we don't know of one that would knock the deer forty feet in the air and drop him on a car windshield like that.
- Most trophies don't have asphalt caked on their antlers.
- Most trophy bucks do not have the local car dealer's emblem branded on their hind quarter.
- Most trophy bucks are three dimensional.
- Most stories of taking a trophy buck do not include "Then I looked down to change the radio station . . ."
- Most trophy bucks don't smell like radiator fluid.

RICK · BUBBA ·

THE ADVANTAGES OF HUNTING WITH A BOW AND ARROW

1. The meat will already be skewered for the barbeque.

2. You won't find a bullet in your sausage.

3. If you miss, you won't have all the other hunters asking, "Hey, I heard a shot. What'd you get?"

4. Arrows are lighter to carry than ammo.

5. If positioned creatively on the crown of the deer, the bows can add to your point count.

6. Since an arrow doesn't travel as fast as a bullet, it prolongs the time between the moment you shoot to the moment you realize you've totally missed your target.

7. The requirements for this type of hunting have changed. You no longer have to wear tights and rob from the rich to give to the poor.

8. You can usually reuse your bows.

9. Arrows rarely ricochet.

10. If you miss, it probably won't bring down a 100-year old pine.

RICK · BUBBA

HOW TO TELL IF A HUNTER IS LYING ABOUT HIS HUNT

1. He closes his story with " . . . And that's when the aliens arrived and took the huge buck away."

2. He says "I was just thinking that the Hartford elk from that insurance commercial would have run with fear from this buck. And then I lost him in my scope."

3. His tale includes any mention of Big Foot.

4. She claims, "I was just shooting up in the air to scare away the lion."

5. The game warden's report quotes him as saying "I just decided to put my gun down and jump on the buck, wrestle it to the ground and break its neck with my bare hands. I don't know where that tire mark came from . . ."

Hunter Bussey shows off large turkey tracks. Or someone in the party is wearing some really funny looking shoes.

6. She says, "The turkey I shot was as big as a SUV, but we can't seem to find him."

7. His lips are moving.

8. She keeps saying ". . . and then uh, the uh, deer, uh ran . . . yeah that's right, he ran that way, then uh, disappeared like a vapor."

9. She says, "I just couldn't shoot the ducks. They seemed too human."

10. He says, "No, I just wear camo because it makes me feel pretty."

TEN THINGS TO DO WITH YOUR EXTRA DEER MEAT

1. Give it as Christmas presents.

2. Feed the dogs for less than those national brands of dog food made from who knows what.

3. Grill it up and throw a block party.

4. Give it to those ladies who make all the Wednesday night church meals. Mmmmm . . . deer meatloaf!

5. Give it to your local school. No more soybean burgers.

6. Have a romantic dinner at home and prepare it for your wife. Nothing says I love you like a deer tenderloin.

7. As a sick joke, make deer jerky with it and have the kids eat it in line while waiting to see Santa.

8. Give it away on the *Rick and Bubba Show*. "Coming up next . . . your chance to win more deer meat!"

9. Donate it to your pastor's family . . . especially if you went hunting on a Sunday instead of going to church.

10. Two words: bambi burgers.

RICK'S MESSAGE TO ALL FATHERS OF DAUGHTERS CONCERNING DEER HEADS ON THE WALL

This is for all of you dads out there who have daughters. I would like to tell you about a 10-point buck whose head hangs on my wall in my home office. He scored 158 on the Boone and Crockett, and other than a slightly surprised look on his face, he is something to behold.

Now, you might think that I've hung this trophy deer in my home office for bragging rights. Or even for nostalgia's sake. But you'd be wrong. I use this deer head for my opening conversation with any young man who desires the company of my only daughter, who is now eighteen years old.

I bring the young man into my office and show him the deer head on the wall and begin the following conversation,

"Son, do you know much about deer hunting?"

The young man will usually answer "No." I then attempt to get him to look at me through the patch of hair that hangs over one eye and makes me feel like I'm talking to a Cyclops. When I feel I have his slightly divided attention, I proceed to tell him the following story. (All dads are welcome to use this story with their own deer head.)

"Son," I begin. "That deer was at one time living a great life. He would run with his guy friends through the woods and swamps, eating acorns and staying in the safety of the deep woods. They would have such fun together and would remain cautious whenever they were moving about in the open, unless under cover of night. They wouldn't ever purposely put themselves in danger. Then son, one day that deer decided to start chasing women." (You may want to pause here for effect). "He chased a woman, otherwise known as a doe, at 3:30 p.m. one sunny afternoon right into an open field where I was sitting in a blind. Then, son, I shot him with my 300 Weatherby rifle right through the heart killing him instantly." (It helps to have your gun handy for presentation. Then, pause once again for effect and say . . .) "Don't end up on the wall, son."

This will usually have your daughter either home thirty minutes earlier than you requested, or the two youngsters will stay home and play Monopoly with you, and you won't ever see him again!

TEN QUESTIONS WE WOULD LIKE TO ASK TOMMY WILCOX

1. Why have we appeared on your show as many times as we have, but have never killed anything worth mounting?

2. Why do the deer seem to know the exact dates of the hunting season? They will skip out in an open

The ultimate father-son outing

field in the middle of the day when it's not hunting season, but as soon as hunting season starts, they're harder to find than Bin Laden.

3. Why is it that when we go somewhere to hunt or fish, people always say "Hey, you should have been here yesterday. Man, there were fish and deer everywhere!" Are you telling the wildlife that we are coming, Tommy?

4. Why is it that bucks during the rut act exactly like men after puberty? Are there no "rut education classes" available?

5. Why does your show require so many sponsors and therefore have so many interruptions? Shouldn't you just charge more per commercial and then run fewer of them? (This same question has been posed to the Super Bowl committee.)

6. Have you ever paid to hunt or fish? How do we get a job like that? Can we have yours?

7. Why do you seem to always catch fish and shoot trophy deer every week? Don't you care about your viewers' feelings of inadequacy?

8. Why do you whisper into the camera as if we can still hear you? We can't hear you without turning up the volume on our television set to full range. But then, at that level, when you fire your gun, it causes eardrum damage. Is this what you're going for? If not, quit your whispering and speak up!

9. Do you really see deer every time you say into the camera "Look, here comes a good buck," or are you just toying with us?

10. Do you ever feel silly driving up to church in your logo-covered truck?

TEN RULES FOR SHOPPING AT A HUNTING STORE

1. No matter how excited you are that hunting season has begun, do not shoot the stuffed game on display in the store. This is overkill and potentially dangerous to the other customers.

2. Never go to a hunting store the day before the beginning of any season. This is when all the rookies are coming in, and since many of these dedicated souls are clueless, the lines will be long and the help will be frustrated.

3. Never buy the clothing that is hanging on a rack outside the store. This is the stuff that nobody else wanted, and that the store is trying to get rid of. You never hear of anyone stealing these items. There is a reason for this. This stuff is guaranteed to make you the laughingstock at the hunting camp. Is that the look you're going for?

4. Never buy any equipment that is on sale. It's often out of date; that's why they've marked it down. It's expired; they need to just throw it out! (. . .wait, that's the rule for milk. Sorry.)

5. When buying a scope for your gun, never buy the most expensive or the least expensive scope. Buy the one in between. The top of the line is no better than the others, but rich people think it is. The

bottom of the line isn't all that great, even if it doubles as a kaleidoscope for those hunts when you're really, really bored. You want to buy the middle-of-the-road kind of scope.

6. Never buy new camo and wear it the same day of your purchase. Not only will it smell, but it will be stiffer than the cardboard it was wrapped around. It creates the same phenomenon as wearing your new blue jeans the first day of school and not being able to sit down in your chair.

7. When buying two-way radios, remember every salesperson will lie to you regarding what the radios can actually do. They may not mean to lie, but two-way radios never cover the distance they say they will. Just accept the fact that you are never going to find two-way radios that will enable you to keep asking all throughout the day "Hey, you seen anything yet?" That's a luxury you will have to do without.

8. Ask the oldest guy working there (bearing in mind that he could be the greeter at the front door) what you should get. He is the only one who really knows what he's talking about. He has been successful and couldn't care less what the latest and greatest is. He already knows what the latest and greatest is from years of experience and would love to tell you all about it

9. Buy a lifetime license if your state offers it, maybe even one that you can pass down to your heirs. It is a nightmare to have to renew your hunting license every year. Anything that will improve this process is a good thing.

10. Tell the hunting store that you will put their logo in the picture of the big buck you kill if they will help you get one . . . if you know what I mean. They all have their favorite hunting locations that they only tell their favorite customers about. In fact, use the same sales person each time you go, if at all possible. You need this guy to understand

your way of doing things, and if you take care of him, he just might take care of you with a little freebie every now and then.

And maybe his secret map.

TEN PLACES TO TELL YOUR WIFE YOU'RE GOING INSTEAD OF SAYING HUNTING

We've already covered the husband's hunting rules and regulations in our first book (*Rick and Bubba's Expert Guide to God, Country, Family . . . and Anything Else We*

Can Think Of). But what we did not cover was where to tell your wife you're going instead of hunting. Please understand us. We are not suggesting that you lie to your wife. For any of you newly married men who don't know this yet, wives are equipped with a built-in lie detector. We don't know why God saw fit to put this in women. Men really could have used it more because it is so much harder for men to tell when their wives are lying. But ours is not to question why. Ours is but to do and not lie. So, no, we are not suggesting that in the least.

But as hunting can sometimes be a divisive word, it may require a more creative way of explaining your upcoming hunting expedition. This bit of verbal stretching is sort of like what your wife does with the children when she takes them for their immunizations and says "This isn't going to hurt a bit." Or when she tells you the meatloaf in the refrigerator is "still good."

With that in mind, here are a few suggestions of what to say as you're loading up the truck for what might appear to her on the surface as a hunting trip:

1. Honey, I want to get you some fresh flowers, and it would mean so much more if I could pick them one-by-one in the wild.

2. I'm going out to look at some land for us to build our dream home. . . . Of course I know it's 3:30 in the morning. But I want to see it at daybreak.

3. I'm going out to get us some dinner. . . . Of course I know it's 3:30 in the morning, but I want to beat the crowds.

4. I'm going to take the kids out with me to give you some time alone. . . . No, I am not delirious.

5. Honey, I want you to know that this weekend I will be doing my part to feed hungry families. *(For those of you who may not be aware of this, Hunters for the Hungry does just that. They accept any donated kill from hunters and will give the food to families in the community who don't have enough to eat. So again, it's all in how you word it.)*

6. I'm going out to be with other men and we'll discuss how to be better husbands and fathers. Stop laughing, you'll wake the children.

7. I'm going out to a peaceful, quiet place where I can think about how much I love you.

8. I'm going to a place of solitude to pray.

9. I'm going to get refreshed so that when I come back, I can help you more with the house and kids. Maybe even do a better job at work and make more money for us. I might even bring about world peace.

10. I'm going to go to a quiet place and contemplate what our next book should be about. The camouflage is to throw off any stalkers.

RICK · BUBBA

THE WINDY COUNTRY

Rick and Bubba Official Disclaimer: We have tried to handle the following story as delicately as possible.

We certainly don't want to embarrass Tommy Wilcox, but he may enjoy a good "wind storm" more than any other grown man we've ever seen. By wind, we're not talking about Dorothy and the Land of Oz (although in some instances there may be a similarity in velocity). The kind of wind we're referring to is "*that* kind of wind." A release of "that kind of wind" will send Tommy into a fit of hysterical

Coach Burgess, Tommy Wilcox, and Rich Wingo leave for the hunt. With hunting buddies who snack on bean dip and tortilla chips all night, open air vehicles are considered best.

laughter the likes of which has never before been heard in human history.

We witnessed that kind of hysteria one night while hunting. It was getting too dark to shoot anything, but there were animals all over the food plot, and all we could do was sit there and watch them taunt us. There were hogs, does, young bucks, and all kinds of critters walking around as if hunting season was long over and it was their time to party. A buck even showed up; but again it was too dark to count his points to determine whether he was big enough to take. To my dismay, all I (Rick) could do was sit in my plastic chair and watch the game moving about in the field.

It was also at that moment that I felt a slight bloating sensation begin to rise in my innermost being. I moved from side to side, trying my best to settle it down, but that only made matters worse; the sensation would not be ignored. It was set on escaping, and the effect was going to be loud. Little did I realize, though, that the plastic chair I was sitting on would act like a BOSE wave speaker system and amplify the noise to eardrum-shattering decibels.

Missiles have made less noise launching. The "wind storm" not only delivered the loudest boom I had ever heard, it echoed off the swamp in the backwoods for at least five minutes. All the animals went running for cover, even the hogs, so you know it had to be bad. It was so bad, the doors on Tommy's truck shut themselves.

The others surrounding me tried waving it off, but to no avail. It was as if their hands hit up against an invisible wall in mid-air. That thing was holding together like a thunder-storm. We, of course, had no way of measuring the intense power of it, but it was clearly one for the Hunter's Wind Hall of Fame.

Needless to say, Tommy lost it. He bent over laughing, and there was absolutely no bringing him back. There was no bringing the animals back either. At least, not for the rest of the night. I could be wrong, but this is probably the reason you never see plastic chairs in a formal dining room.

TEN REASONS DEER HUNTING IS BENEFICIAL FOR YOUR HEALTH

1. It helps you to catch up on much needed sleep.

2. It helps your body recover from the unnatural daily grind of being responsible.

3. It gives your pores much needed fresh air.

4. Hiking to your hunting house, or climbing up to your tree stand, works your gluteus maximus.

5. Climbing up to a tree stand is an awesome workout for your quads and calves.

6. A shotgun blast close up clears the ears better than a fistful of cotton swabs.

7. Eating whatever you want on an unsupervised (no wives) hunting trip cleanses the digestive system.

8. Shooting things is good for your fine motor skills.

9. Putting your equipment, snacks, and stuff out in your shooting house is sort of like doing curls.

10. Quail, duck, deer, turkey, dove—they are all free range organic food. And they're free.

RICK AND BUBBA'S SONGS FOR THE HUNTER

Note: Use your own discretion on whether you sing along with these.

Songs for Before the Hunt:

All I Have to Do is Dream, The Everly Brothers

Our Day Will Come, Ruby and the Romantics

Always On My Mind, Willie Nelson

Taylor Burgess (16) gets his first buck. Rick's brother and Taylor's dad, Greg Burgess (pictured in back), Rich Wingo (to Taylor's left), Tommy Wilcox (to Taylor's right).   Rick's buck was too big to fit in the photo.

Songs for When Your Wife Won't Let You Go:

Why, Lady, Why?, Alabama

Don't Go Breakin' My Heart, Elton John and Kiki Dee

He Stopped Loving Her Today, George Jones

Don't it Make My Brown Eyes Blue, Crystal Gayle

Help Me Make it Through the Night, Sammi Smith

Sleeping Single in a Double Bed, Barbara Mandrell

Hard Headed Woman, Elvis Presley

I Beg Of You, Elvis Presley

Devil Woman, Cliff Richard

Hurt So Bad, Linda Ronstadt

Release Me, Engelbert Humperdinck

Ain't 2 Proud 2 Beg, The Temptations

Everything I Do I Do It for You, Bryan Adams

**Songs for Planning Your Early Morning
    Escape:**

Coward of the County, Kenny Rogers

A Lesson in Leavin', Dottie West

Runaway, Del Shannon

Easier Said Than Done, The Essex

Songs for When Your Wife Finally Relents:

A Good Hearted Woman, Waylon Jennings

Oh, What a Night, The Four Seasons

I Will Always Love You, Whitney Houston

Kiss An Angel Good Morning, Charley Pride

She Believes in Me, Kenny Rogers

I Honestly Love You, Olivia Newton John

Celebration, Kool & The Gang

The Hallelujah Chorus, Handel

Songs for the Morning of the Hunt:

Tossin' and Turnin', Bobby Lewis

It's Four in the Morning, Faron Young

Lord, I Hope This Day Is Good, Don Williams

High Hopes, Frank Sinatra

Follow That Dream, Elvis Presley

Everything is Beautiful, Ray Stevens

Somewhere Out There, James Ingram and Linda
  Ronstadt

All My Rowdy Friends Are Coming Over Tonight,
  Hank Williams, Jr.

Songs for Looking for Your Hunting Spot

I Go Out Walking After Midnight, Patsy Cline

The Wild Side of Life, Hank Thompson

Wild Thing, The Troggs

I'm Walkin' , Fats Domino

In the Still of the Night, The Five Satins

The Wanderer, Dion

These Boots Are Made for Walking, Nancy Sinatra

Ain't No Mountain High Enough, Diana Ross

From A Distance, Bette Midler

Wide Open Spaces, The Dixie Chicks

Lead Me On, Conway Twitty

Songs to Sing From the Tree Stand:

Please Help Me I'm Falling, Hank Locklin

You Keep Me Hanging On, The Supremes

We're Gonna Hold On, George Jones and Tammy Wynette

Hang On Sloopy, the McCoys

Rainy Night in Georgia, Brook Benton

Raindrops Keep Falling On My Head, B. J. Thomas

Against the Wind, Bob Seger & The Silver Bullet

Ain't No Sunshine, Bill Withers

Songs for the Hunting House That Hasn't Been Used in Awhile:

I've Got a Tiger By the Tail, Buck Owens

The Lion Sleeps Tonight, The Tokens

Crocodile Rock, Elton John

Me and My Shadow, Frank Sinatra

Jeepers Creepers, Louis Armstrong

*The Darkest Hour Is Just Before Dawn, Emmylou
  Harris*

I'm Gonna Sleep With One Eye Open, Dolly Parton

I'm So Lonesome I Could Cry, Hank Williams

Oh, Lonesome Me, Don Gibson

We Gotta Get Out of This Place, The Animals

I Will Survive, Gloria Gaynor

Sitting, Waiting, Wishing, Jack Johnson

Songs for When The Deer is Taunting You:

Here You Come Again, Dolly Parton

Hit Me With Your Best Shot, Pat Benatar

Everybody Plays the Fool, The Main Ingredient

Stay, SugarLand

Un-break My Heart, Toni Braxton

The Heart Is a Lonely Hunter, Reba McEntire

Songs for the Ones That Get Away

I'll Get Over You, Crystal Gayle

Please Don't Go, KC and the Sunshine Band

Wake Me Up Before You Go-Go, Wham!

Cry, Cry, Cry, Johnny Cash

Songs for When You Come Home Empty-Handed:

What Becomes of the Brokenhearted?, Jimmy Ruffin

Didn't We Almost Have It All?, Whitney Houston

Stand By Your Man, Tammy Wynette

I Won't Mention It Again, Ray Price

Rub it In, Billy "Crash" Craddock

Some Broken Hearts Never Mend, Don Williams

Don't Cry, Daddy, Elvis Presley

Wasted Days and Wasted Nights, Freddy Fender

How Am I Supposed to Live Without You?, Michael
    Bolton

If I Could Turn Back Time, Cher

Born to Lose, Ray Charles

Another Time, Another Place, Sandi Patty

Achy Breaky Heart, Billy Ray Cyrus

My Heart Will Go On, Celine Dion

**Songs for When You Come Home with a
Trophy Buck:**

O, Lord, It's Hard to Be Humble, Mac Davis

Dancing in the Street, Martha and the Vandellas

I'm So Excited, the Pointer Sisters

Something to Talk About, Bonnie Raitt

Another One Bites the Dust, Queen

You Make Me Feel Like Dancing, Leo Sayer

For Once In My Life, Stevie Wonder

I Could Not Ask For More, Sara Evans

You Are So Beautiful, Joe Cocker

Celebrate, Kool and the Gang

Songs for Accidentally Bagging a Spike

Shame, Shame, Shame, Jimmy Reed

Singing the Blues, Marty Robbins

A Fool Such As I, Elvis Presley

I Got Stung, Elvis Presley

I Am A Man of Constant Sorrow, the Soggy Bottom Boys version

Hard to Say I'm Sorry, Chicago

In the Jailhouse Now, the Soggy Bottom Boys version

RICK • BUBBA •

TEN WAYS TO WORK A HUNTING TRIP INTO THE FAMILY SCHEDULE

1. "Hey, guys, let's go camping for quality family time together . . . and say, while we're there, who's up for hunting?"

2. Plan a father/son or a father/daughter hunting birthday party for your offspring's special day. Mom will love watching you and your heir dress out a deer before sitting down for a little cake and ice cream. Make sure there is a party hat for the deer, too.

3. Tell Mom you will take the kids hunting to give her a break (this is almost foolproof). Be prepared to cram kids into a shooting house, and remember to bring lots of snacks.

4. Have a turkey hunt on your way to work. Who will know? Sure, when you show up at the office with your face painted in camo people will talk, but tell them it's some sort of theme day.

5. Tell your wife "Hey, honey, we should all eat dinner together more often." Tonight I will cook a meal for all of us . . . right after I kill it!

6. Make your Little League end of the season party a hunting theme. "Hey guys, Coach Rick is going to hunt for a little while and bring in a nice buck,

and then we will hand out this season's Little League trophies."

7. Take the wife out for a much-deserved retreat in a beautiful shooting house over-looking a breathtaking green field. "Honey, we can spend hours looking into each other's eyes, whispering how much we love each other . . . until one hour before dark when we have to be completely quiet and think about our future while looking through a pair of binoculars."

8. "Honey, do you need me to go hunting this weekend to get refreshed so I can think about how to be more understanding?"

9. "Honey, I think I will take the boys somewhere after school and get their homework done before we get home."

10. "Honey, I have a great idea for something the boys could carry to show and tell . . . how about deer antlers? Wouldn't that be cool, guys?"

WHY A FORK IS NOT A GOOD HUNTING WEAPON

1. It doesn't have a scope.

2. It's hard to kill a huge buck at 200 yards with it.

3. It makes you appear too anxious.

4. What will you use to eat your mac and cheese?

5. If you miss, you could jab yourself with it.

6. The sun reflecting off of it could mess up your photo.

7. Even if you figured out a way to load it, it'd still look funny.

8. It requires mounting the deer.

9. It doesn't have the same zing as a 300 Weatherby.

10. It annoys the deer.

Speedy, Tyler, and J.C. pose for a photo op.
Is that Big Foot behind them . . . again?

RICK AND BUBBA'S HUNTER'S BILL OF RIGHTS

1. All hunters will receive a tax exemption on every item used for hunting, including the truck. This is only fair, due to the fact that we are doing the government a service by feeding people through Hunting for Food Banks programs, as well as

managing the deer herd for our home states. (Hey, if we're paying farmers not to grow food, why not do something to help us hunters out, too?)

2. Each hunter shall have the right to several days off of work to hunt. These "hunting days" shall not count against normal vacation time. It is a shame to watch the families of hunters lose valuable family time because Daddy had to use his vacation days for hunting.

3. Every hunter with a wife and children has the right to a minimum of four guilt-free hunts per season. These are different than the above work days. These days will be on the hunter's normal days off and will be mutually agreed upon by the wife. However, once set, the hunter cannot be made to feel guilty about going.

4. Any hunting trips made on a Sunday shall count as the equivalent of going to church. (Look, it's quiet, God is there, and you plainly see His creation firsthand. Also, if you're lucky enough to see

an 8-point buck run into the clearing, you do an awful lot of praying while you're trying to get him in your sights.)

5. Wives will accept dues and/or fees paid to the hunting club as a need, not a want, and they will not be allowed to bring up the name of Dave Ramsey during any discussion on the matter.

6. Hunters shall have the right to wear camo to work (even if it's not casual Friday) in order to be able to leave quickly for an afternoon hunt. It's all about efficiency.

7. When you wear camo to work, positively no one at work can use the worn out phrase "Hey, I didn't see you there." This comment makes no sense. Now, if the hunter was wearing the pattern of the office, then we could understand this saying. But most offices aren't wallpapered with camo, and thus the line "Hey, I didn't see you there" is inappropriate.

8. During turkey season, the work day will be changed to begin at 11 a.m. local time. This later starting

time allows for a little early morning hunting, as well as getting the pictures developed at the one-hour photo place.

9. Dads have the right to aim and shoot at the same trophy buck their sons are aiming at, if in their advance wisdom and experience they determine that the shot might require more expertise and back-up.

10. All hunters shall have unlimited bragging rights, without fear of or demand for substantiation. The hunter's description of the buck that got away shall be the official record. No ifs, ands, or buts.

RICK AND BUBBA'S HUNTER HALL OF FAME CERTIFICATE

WHEREAS _____, a hunter of the finest order, has faithfully and dutifully handled his weapon and himself to the best of his ability on the hunting fields of the United States;

WHEREAS, due to his unfailing love for his beautiful wife and family, he has tried not to wake them whenever he has left the house at three o'clock in the morning, especially if the hunting trip is a surprise to everyone but him;

WHEREAS, due to his commitment to his family and his country, said hunter has sacrificed his weekends to go out and fight against the harsh elements, to go without home cooked meals, to relieve himself in places that would make a public restroom seem like an operating room, all to help manage the deer population of his community;

WHEREAS, his sense of duty has made him think only of his wonderful wife and loving family, whom he missed and thought of often while in the hunting houses of America, and who, because of his sacrifice, are now blessed with some of the finest meat that money could not buy;

WHEREAS, to prove his love for those around him, and to prepare for this supreme sacrifice, he has spent money that he labored for on such necessities as a rifle, scope, binoculars, camo, a four-wheeler, and boots (not to mention the snacks);

WHEREAS, to provide the best possible chance to achieve his goal, he has selected the best hunting houses or tree stands for himself. This has, by no means, been a selfish act. He needed to have a better hunting house and tree stand than the other hunters because of his duty to all the aforementioned dependents;

WHEREAS, the above-mentioned hunter has proved his superb aim and has rarely missed his target, except for the following occasion when instead of the _____ that he was aiming for, he hit (circle one):

    a. a tree

    b. the guide truck

    c. the backside of his hunting partner

    d. (other)_____;

WHEREAS, this hunter has never once shirked from his responsibility to show up on the hunting field at the appointed time;

We do hereby induct _____ into the

Rick and Bubba Hunter's Hall of Fame on this _____ day of the month of _____ in the year of our Lord 20_____ .

THE LAST WILL AND TESTAMENT OF RICK BURGESS

I, Rick Burgess, being of sound mind and nearly sound body, do hereby will that all my earthly possessions of a hunting persuasion be distributed in the following manner:

My gun, the 300 Remington (known in hunting circles as "Black death"), shall be given to my brother Greg Burgess.

This is due to the fact that he has always claimed that something is wrong with this very gun that he has borrowed over the years, and thus could be the reason he has an unusual amount of misses. If the gun is his, he will be free to have it checked out to his heart's content. This should once and for all clear his suspicion and my reputation. It will be the last time he will get to utter those infamous words, "I wonder if it's the gun."

I would like my favorite camo outfit to be placed on a slightly overweight mannequin and placed in my home office, directly under my 10-point deer head to remind my wife of how good I looked in camo.

If it isn't too much trouble, even though I have passed on, I would really like for my wife to place my remaining deer heads somewhere where people can actually see them as soon as the enter our home . . . perhaps along the staircase as you enter the house. If people have to duck, then they have to duck—for the sake of sentimentality.

I would like for my remaining camo to be altered for a person of Bubba's height and given to him to use as he wills. I think Bubba wears a 29-length.

My remaining pairs of boots that have been given to me by some of the finest hunting lines in the world should be bronzed and placed at my favorite hunting spots, just to the right if you were facing the shooting house or ladder stand. A brief ceremony would be appropriate.

My four-wheelers should be given to my children, but only if they agree to continue the family tradition of hunting. There is no better way to tell Dad that you love him than by doing your part to manage the herd of the great whitetail deer.

My children should continue to petition the State of Alabama in which I was born, raised, worked, hunted, and have now passed from, to move the dates of deer season so that bow hunting starts in November and gun hunting begins in mid-December and continues through February. It could be a tough battle, but I feel they are up to the challenge.

I leave my shotgun to my oldest son to use to scare and threaten any guys who want to date or marry his sister and my only daughter.

Our farm should go to my wife who is free to continue to make it a great place to fish and hunt for the boys, but it should be ripped from her if she ever becomes remarried to a man who doesn't hunt or fish . . . or make that if she gets remarried at all (this is because the guy might just be saying he hunts. Guys lie. Women do, too. They might both be in on the hoax.)

Finally, I will that my deer grunts be buried with me. These have been in my mouth . . . no one else can use them. If you want a Rick and Bubba souvenir, take this book on up to the counter and buy it. You've been standing there in the aisle thumbing through it long enough.

THE LAST WILL AND TESTAMENT OF BUBBA BUSSEY

Ditto what Rick said.

CLOSING THOUGHTS

Well, there you have it—the last word on hunting. We set out to tell you everything we knew about the sport of hunting . . . and a few things we didn't. We hope we've accomplished that, and that you've had some fun with us along the way.

You know, both of us feel blessed to have plenty of good memories of time spent with our dads hunting, fishing, and playing sports. These are memories that neither one of us would trade for all the money in the world.

Now that we each have kids of our own, we're continuing

the tradition of taking our offspring along with us on many of our hunting trips. We've had some incredible bonding times together. We've laughed, and we've even cried a few times (when we've missed a shot). But on each trip one thing is for certain—we were making memories.

In today's society, fathers are too often discounted and disrespected, especially as they're portrayed on some television shows or in commercials. But a dad is one of the most important influences in the life of a son or daughter.

Whatever sport or hobby you and your kids enjoy doing together, or that you and your own father take pleasure in, we encourage you to make the time to do it. Don't get so busy trying to provide for your family that you forget to spend quality time with them. Children need their dads. And dads, even after their children are all grown up, still enjoy spending time with their kids. Outdoor sports are a great way to make sure that happens.

So, make the effort. Life is too short. Start a tradition in your own family of something you enjoy doing together. Your kids will thank you for it. And you just might end up with some of the best memories of your life. (Not to mention some trophy bucks).

RICK AND BUBBA'S GLOSSARY OF HUNTING TERMS

8-point buck: nickname for a pastor friend of ours who loves to hunt but doesn't realize that all good Baptist preachers should only have three points.

binoculars: used by the most skilled hunters to determine how many points the buck who just walked out into the open has on his head; also used to spy on other hunters back at the lodge to see if someone is stealing your snacks from your backpack.

Bobo no-no: doing something that you should not be doing; (Inspired by a similar phrase, "Bozo no-no" from the old *Bozo the Clown* television show.)

Book of Blame: imaginary reference used primarily by spouses to shift responsibility for a bad event; often referenced when a clear shot is missed.

The Bubbarosa: the large spread owned by Bubba where various and sundry outdoor recreational activities are possible (also known as Big Lick Farm).

Buck Nelson: a prize deer, perhaps even an unattainable one; term apparently coined by Greg Burgess.

deer grunt call: what my (Rick) wife does to get me to take out the garbage.

deer hunting season: the time when real men only pretend to be interested in things outside of hunting deer. It is also the time when even on a date with your wife, you ask the waiter if he has seen any good bucks around lately.

deer tracks: what a true hunter sees everywhere he goes, including at church and sometimes in his own closet.

feeding area: the area right outside the kitchen door of the hunting lodge; often the perfect setting to find the great overweight hunter.

field dressing: putting on your camo about halfway to your deer stand when you realize you have rushed out of the lodge in your underwear after oversleeping.

rattle bag: used by big-time hunters to give the impression of two bucks fighting to lure in a big buck; can also be used to frustrate the drive-thru employee when stopping for a bite on the way home with your hunting buddies.

scent-free hunting: something most hunters talk about, but due to eating bacon, sausage, double cheeseburgers with onions, standing and telling stories around the fire, etc. is never ever achieved; such scent violations often contribute to the majority of harvested deer being those with sinus infections

shooting house: a small place where hunters escape the responsibilities of the real world and think of nothing but hunting, protected from questions from small children, wives, and anyone from work; very similar to his home bathroom.

trophy buck: the one that only you saw but couldn't get a decent shot at; also the one you shot, but that got away, and *not* this other deer lying on the ground.

venison cutlets: the original free range organic meat (deer hunters were organic long before the hippies).

whitetail deer: what true hunters count when trying to go to sleep on the night before the big hunt.